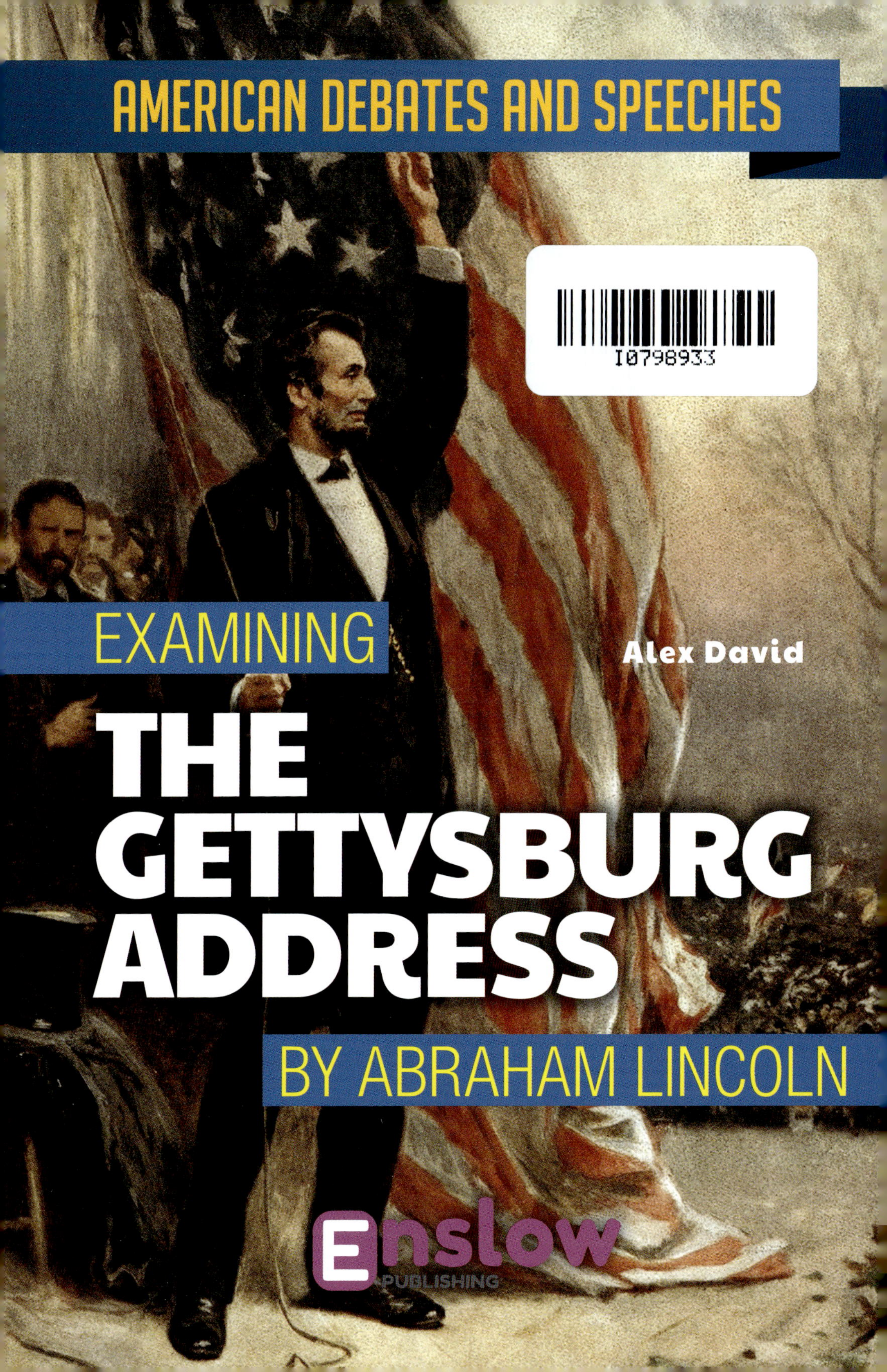

AMERICAN DEBATES AND SPEECHES

EXAMINING THE GETTYSBURG ADDRESS BY ABRAHAM LINCOLN

Alex David

Enslow PUBLISHING

Published in 2021 by Enslow Publishing, LLC
101 W. 23rd Street, Suite 240, New York, NY 10011

Library of Congress Cataloging-in-Publication Data

Names: David, Alex, author.

Title: Examining the Gettysburg Address by Abraham Lincoln / Alex David.
Description: New York, NY : Enslow Publishing, 2021. | Series: American debates and speeches | Includes bibliographical references and index. | Audience: Grades 6-12.
Identifiers: LCCN 2019014895| ISBN 9781978515161 (library bound) | ISBN 9781978515154 (pbk.)
Subjects: LCSH: Lincoln, Abraham, 1809-1865. Gettysburg address. | Lincoln, Abraham, 1809-1865. | Speeches, addresses, etc., American--History and criticism. | United States--History--Civil War, 1861-1865--Causes. | Soldiers' National Cemetery (Gettysburg, Pa.)
Classification: LCC E475.55 .D38 2020 | DDC 973.7092--dc23
LC record available at https://lccn.loc.gov/2019014895

To Our Readers: We have done our best to make sure all websites in this book were active and appropriate when we went to press. However, the author and the publisher have no control over and assume no liability for the material available on those websites or on any websites they may link to. Any comments or suggestions can be sent by email to customerservice@enslow.com.

Portions of this book originally appeared in *Lincoln's Gettyburg Address: A Primary Source Investigation* by Steven P. Olsen

Photos Credits: Photo research by Bruce Donnola

Cover, pp. 1, 51 Everett Historical/Shutterstock.com; p. 5 Library of Congress, Robert Todd Lincoln Papers, Manuscript Division; pp. 8, 23, 55 Corbis Historical/Getty Images; p. 11 Kean Collection/Archive Photos/Getty Images; p. 17 National Portrait Gallery, London, UK/De Agostini Picture Library/Bridgeman Images; p. 18 Library of Congress Prints and Photographs Division; p. 24 John Greim/LightRocket/Getty Images; p. 28 PhotoQuest/Archive Photos/Getty Images; p. 30 Tom Leonard/Conde Nast Collection/Getty Images; p. 33 Hulton Archive/Archive Photos/Getty Images; p. 38 Buyenlarge/Archive Photos/Getty Images; p. 39 John Frost Newspapers/Alamy Stock Photo; p. 41 Karen Bleier/AFP/Getty Images; pp. 42, 45, 54 Universal History Archive/Universal Images Group/Getty Images; p. 46 Archive Photos/Getty Images; p. 50 Bettmann/Getty Images; Ozz Design/Shutterstock.com (back cover and interior pages background pattern); pashabo/Shutterstock.com (interior pages American flag patterns); Midwaves/Shutterstock.com, Leonid Zarubin/Shutterstock.com (interior pages abstract textures and patterns)

CONTENTS

INTRODUCTION

Abraham Lincoln was not the first choice to speak at the Soldiers' National Cemetery ceremony. The organizer, David Wills, wanted a poet like Henry Wadsworth Longfellow to consecrate the land where so many soldiers had died. However, Longfellow said no. Wills asked other poets: John Greenleaf Whittier and William Cullen Bryant. They both said no. Wills asked General Meade, but he also said no. Wills had already gotten the "best orator of the day," Edward Everett, to speak, but he needed someone else. The Gettysburg battle was the bloodiest battle of the Civil War. The cemetery would inter (place in a grave) 3,512 bodies. There needed to be a ceremony. Wills wanted speakers who would make the sacred ground they were standing on special. On November 2, Wills sent a letter to Abraham Lincoln. Lincoln said yes.

Edward Everett spoke for two hours. Abraham Lincoln spoke for about two minutes. He said 272 words. The language was not difficult. Most of the words were one or two syllables. And, yet, Lincoln was able to deliver a speech that not only spoke to the people at the ceremony, not only to the divided nation, but to us now—people in the twenty-first century. The Gettysburg Address endures. It continues to teach and remind us what our country was founded on, what the sacrifices of war were for.

Perhaps, Wills did get a poet to speak. President Lincoln's words weren't the romantic verse of Longfellow, but they were certainly poetic. On November 19, 1863, Lincoln poetically called for the nation to do "the unfinished work which they who fought here have thus far so nobly advanced." Everett later wrote to Lincoln,"Permit me . . . to express my great admiration of the thoughts expressed by you, with such eloquent simplicity and appropriateness, at the consecration of the Cemetery. I should be glad, if I could flatter myself that I came as near to the central idea of the occasion, in two hours, as you did in two minutes."

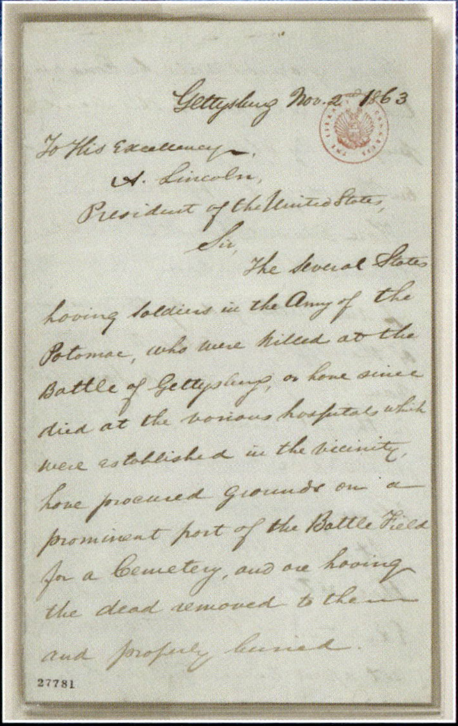

Gettysburg Nov. 2nd 1863

To His Excellency
A. Lincoln,
President of the United States,
Sir,
The several States having soldiers in the Army of the Potomac, who were killed at the Battle of Gettysburg, or have since died at the various hospitals which were established in the vicinity, have procured grounds on a prominent part of the Battle Field for a Cemetery, and are having the dead removed to them and properly buried.

27781

Here is the letter from David Wills asking President Lincoln to speak at Gettysburg in 1863.

Ideas were precisely the reason why Lincoln's speech was so important. Lincoln drew listeners' attention, not to the Constitution, but to the Declaration of Independence: "all men are created equal." Now, we hold the Gettysburg Address as a pillar of our country. In the Lincoln Memorial in Washington, DC, the Gettysburg Address is written on the walls.

The speech about those who died in battle has become more famous than the battle itself, perhaps because the speech gave meaning to the battle. Lincoln was able to summarize why the war was so important. He gave meaning to why the dead had died. They gave their lives so that the idea of America could exist. Freedom for everyone was more important than their individual lives. They, like Lincoln, believed in the concept of America. A country's government should be for the people and by the people. Democracy can exist. Lincoln's address may have been short, but it rang large. To truly understand these 272 words, we must understand the unique man and the devastating war that led to the Gettysburg Address.

CHAPTER ONE

THE EARLY LIFE OF ABRAHAM LINCOLN

The Gettysburg Address was written by a president with only one year of formal schooling. Abraham Lincoln was born on February 12, 1809, in Hodgenville, Kentucky. He lived in a one room log cabin on the south fork of Nolin Creek. His family had moved to Kentucky from Virginia, in hopes of finding better farmland. However, they struggled in Kentucky. The family moved to Indiana. Lincoln's mother died when he was only eight years old.

After his mother's death, Lincoln's chores around the house increased and kept him home from school. As the only son, Lincoln was expected to help his father with the farming. In Indiana, he was sent to a school that opened about a mile (1.6 kilometers) from the family farm, but it closed three months later. By the time he was fifteen, Lincoln's formal education was over. He had attended school for just one year.

Thirst for Knowledge

Somehow, Lincoln managed to learn to read. His stepmother, Sarah Bush Lincoln, owned a few books. Although she could

In 1861, Abraham Lincoln became the 16th president of the United States.

not read or write, she sensed that schooling was important and encouraged Lincoln to read. Between chores, Lincoln read *Pilgrim's Progress* by John Bunyan, *Aesop's Fables*, or the family Bible. As quoted in *The Hidden Lincoln: From the Letters and Papers of William H. Herndon*, Sarah Bush Lincoln later recalled,

> He [Lincoln] must understand everything, even to the smallest thing, minutely and exactly; he would then repeat it over to himself again and again, sometimes in one form and then in another, and when it was fixed in his mind to suit him he became easy and he never lost that fact or his understanding of it.

As Lincoln became more involved in reading and learning, his work around the farm suffered. His father knew that Lincoln was not meant to be a farmer. By the time he left home at eighteen, Lincoln had grown to six feet four inches tall (1.9 meters). He had only one total year of schooling, yet he possessed a burning desire to be something other than a farmer.

Lincoln's Draw to Politics

Lincoln's next few years were spent in search of a career. While learning to survey the Illinois countryside, to pilot riverboats, and to manage a country store, Lincoln discovered an interest in politics and an ability to speak publicly. A very tall man for the time, he drew attention wherever he spoke. To his thoughtful speeches given around Illinois, he often added colorful tales of growing up in the country.

Encouraged by friends and admirers in the town of New Salem, Lincoln ran for the Illinois state legislature in 1832. Although he lost, he ran again in 1834 and won. Lincoln was faced with the challenge of creating laws in the state legislature. He responded by borrowing the books of a friend and began studying the law in earnest. Three years later, Lincoln was a licensed attorney and a two-term member of the state legislature.

Lincoln's Art of Storytelling

Lincoln was known as a storyteller. Growing up he listened to the adults tell stories to one another. Soon, he memorized not only what they said, but also how they said it. He became infatuated with communication at a young age, understanding that a good speaker both teaches and entertains their listeners.

In the 19th century, it was common for orators to travel around to different towns and tell stories. Although today speakers often use TED Talk stages, speakers in the 1800s would use tree stumps or the back of wagons.

Lincoln began to get a reputation for his skills as a storyteller. People liked to listen to him. Although he had a calm temperament, his stories were jovial and humorous. Lincoln understood the charisma that is needed to command an audience. This was certainly true in the Gettysburg Address.

This illustration shows the soon to be president, Abraham Lincoln, walking with detective Allan Pinkerton and lawyer, Ward Hill Lamon in 1861.

A Man of Promise

At a friend's party in 1839, Lincoln met a small, bright-eyed twenty-two-year-old woman named Mary Todd. Todd came from a prosperous banking family in Lexington, Kentucky. Although this smart and lively woman had little in common with the country-born Lincoln, Mary Todd saw that he was a man of promise. They married on November 4, 1842. The following August, their first child, Robert Todd Lincoln, was born. The Lincolns had three more sons, Edward, Willie, and Tad.

The Path to President

During the 1830s, Lincoln joined the Whig political party. Founded in 1830 under the leadership of Henry Clay and Daniel Webster, the Whigs supported tariffs to protect US industries, the formation of a national bank, and a conservative policy for selling public lands. As the main alternative to the Democratic Party at the time, the Whig Party gained popularity throughout the 1830s. Lincoln supported its policies and candidates as a member of the Illinois legislature.

In 1841, Lincoln returned from the legislature and resumed practicing law in Springfield, Illinois, with Stephen F. Logan, a prominent and capable attorney. In court, Logan was responsible for preparing the case, while Lincoln used simple words, homey stories, and a conversational style to speak to juries. Their legal practice thrived.

Yet politics still called to Lincoln. In part because they both wanted to run for the US Congress, Lincoln and Logan dissolved their partnership in 1844. Although the Democrats had a strong majority in Illinois, the Seventh Congressional District, in which Lincoln lived, supported the Whigs. Lincoln failed to secure the Whig nomination for Congress in 1844. However, his good speeches around the district and hard work for the Whig Party were recognized. In his work as a lawyer, he continued to travel throughout central Illinois and to develop political contacts. Two years later, he won a seat in Congress.

Lincoln and his family headed to Washington. In national politics for the first time, Congressman Lincoln had to address the issue of slavery. As it divided the nation, so too did it divide the House of Representatives and the Northern and Southern Whig Party members.

Among the many opinions in the Whig Party, Lincoln's voice was a moderate one. Concerning the issue of slavery, Lincoln believed that if its expansion was prevented, it would naturally die out in the South. According to David Donald in *Lincoln*, the future president wrote in an 1845 letter:

> I hold it to be a paramount duty of us in the free states, due to the Union of the states, and perhaps to liberty itself . . . to let the slavery of the other states alone; while, on the other hand, I hold it to be equally clear, that we should never knowingly lend ourselves directly or indirectly, to prevent that slavery from dying a natural death.

More than ending slavery, Lincoln believed in the wholeness of the United States, suggesting that he "would consent to the extension of it [slavery] rather than see the Union dissolved." His patience and priorities would later carry him through the Civil War.

In 1848, Congressman Lincoln campaigned in Maryland, Massachusetts, and Illinois on behalf of the Whig candidate for president, General Zachary Taylor. Lincoln urged Taylor to support the Wilmot Proviso, a bill in Congress that would have outlawed the extension of slavery into new territories. However, there was strong opposition to the bill, which eventually failed, and Lincoln focused on campaigning for Taylor.

In part because of Lincoln's efforts, Taylor was elected in 1848, but he died in office in 1850. With the deaths of founders Clay and Webster in 1852, the Whig Party collapsed. That year, its presidential candidate, General Winfield Scott, won only four states in the election. Southern Whigs split off, and many joined the Democratic Party.

The Lincoln-Douglas Debates

In 1854, Illinois senator Stephen Douglas, a Democratic rival of Lincoln's, sponsored the Kansas-Nebraska Bill. Its aim was to allow slavery in the Kansas and Nebraska territories, which were far north of the border between the North and South. Considered a compromise by Douglas to Southern Democrats, the Kansas-Nebraska Act was forced through Congress. In the state of Illinois, the new law caused great debate, as southern parts of the state were farther south than some slave states. On May 29, 1856, roughly 270 delegates met in Springfield to organize a new political party to oppose the Kansas-Nebraska Act. The delegates were former members of several different parties. Lincoln played a large role in organizing the delegates of what would become the Illinois Republican Party. He was asked to give the final speech of the convention.

Two years later, the Republican Party had officially formed, and Lincoln, a Republican candidate, faced Douglas in Illinois in a senatorial election. During the campaign, the two candidates engaged in seven debates in which Lincoln stood firm in his conviction that slavery should not be spread and that "a house divided against itself cannot stand." Although Lincoln did well in the final three debates, Douglas was reelected.

However, the experience had been good for Lincoln. He was well prepared in 1860 when he ran for president.

CHAPTER TWO

THE CIVIL WAR

In 1860, slavery was on many Americans' minds. Although there were abolitionists arguing for enslaved people to be free, many people thought it should be up to individual states to decide whether slavery was legal in their state. They used the Tenth Amendment to the US Constitution to justify their feelings: "The powers not delegated to the United States by the Constitution, nor prohibited by it to the states, are reserved to the states respectively, or to the people."

How was this amendment to be interpreted? What did the writers of the Constitution intend? Was slavery, which had not yet been outlawed by the US government, to be decided by individual states or the people? Or, did the Declaration of Independence, written eleven years before the Constitution, already free the slaves with its statement that "all men are created equal"? When new states such as California entered the Union, was slavery to be legal, illegal, or decided by the individual state?

Each political party had its own answers to these questions, and some of those answers were bitterly opposed by other parties. Even before the election, it was clear that war was a distinct possibility.

This painting by Benjamin Robert Haydon shows the 1840 convention of the British and Foreign Anti-Slavery Society.

Lincoln Elected President

Before the presidential election of 1860, Lincoln was barely known outside of Illinois. During the presidential campaign, his supporters carried two rails that Lincoln supposedly split as a young man. The legend of "the Rail-Splitter" from out west was born, and a more moderate candidate was presented to the nation. The Northern Democrats nominated Stephen Douglas, while the Southern Democrats nominated the vice president, John C. Breckinridge of Kentucky, who was a

This photograph shows Abraham Lincoln as president.

defender of slavery. John Bell of Tennessee was nominated by the Constitutional Union Party, which had been formed before the election by conservatives who wanted to preserve the Union and its Constitution.

On November 6, 1860, Lincoln was elected president by winning every state in which slavery was illegal, except for New Jersey. He carried no Southern states and earned only 40 percent of the popular vote. The remaining 60 percent was divided among the many other parties and their candidates.

After the election, events began to happen very quickly. Acting on an earlier threat, South Carolina voted to secede from the Union on December 20, 1860. Within two months, Mississippi, Florida, Alabama, Georgia, Louisiana, and Texas followed. On February 8, delegates from Southern states met to adopt a provisional constitution for the Confederate states. At 4:30 a.m. on April 12, 1861, negotiations for a peaceful surrender of Fort Sumter failed, and Brigadier General P. G. T. Beauregard of the Confederate army gave the order to open fire with fifty cannons. The Civil War had begun.

States Secede

By the end of April, seventeen states, with a combined population of nine million people, had joined the Confederate States of America. While the Union had more soldiers, the first battles outside of Washington, DC, confirmed that the war would be long and difficult. At places like Shiloh, Bull Run, and Antietam, the Confederate army under the direction of Generals Robert E. Lee, Stonewall Jackson, and James Longstreet showed considerable skill and resistance. Union forces failed to manage

Lincoln's Sad Demeanor

Although Lincoln told jovial stories, he was often described as having a sad or somber demeanor. An observer commented "his face was the saddest I ever looked upon." In the twenty-first century, we might wonder if Lincoln were depressed. He did have episodes of depression in his life and the Civil War undoubtedly added stress and sadness to his life as president. However, in this role, he never let gloom debilitate him. He was an incredibly even tempered person. Historian Doris Kearns Goodwin describes his temperament as melancholic. Lincoln fully understood his moods and was able to not only rally himself during times of strife, but could also lift the spirits of his colleagues. The Civil War was an anxiety-producing time and Lincoln was able to use humor and language to reassure those around him. Perhaps, this resilience was part of the reason he was such a tremendous president.

more than small gains in the South. Tens of thousands of men on both sides died over the next two years.

The Bloodiest Battle

On June 3, 1863, General Lee's Army of Northern Virginia launched a second invasion of the North. Meanwhile, the 95,000 Union soldiers of the Northern Army of the Potomac were stationed near Washington, DC, to protect the capital. Instead of attacking the capital, Lee headed for the lush farmlands of southern Pennsylvania, which would provide food for his large army. He knew that if he could resupply his army, he would have a chance to squeeze off Washington from other cities and force Lincoln to begin negotiations for a truce. He also wanted to draw the Union army away from Virginia, since it was in position on the Rappahannock River to make a concentrated effort to take Richmond.

Major General George G. Meade of the Union knew that Confederates were nearby, so he ordered Major General John Buford and 2,500 soldiers to scout to the west. They were followed by a larger body of soldiers under the command of Major General John Reynolds.

On June 30, Buford's party rode through gentle hills into the prosperous farming town of Gettysburg. Stopping at the city cemetery on top of a hill, Buford spied a half dozen Confederate flags at the center of town. A Confederate soldier took a shot at Buford's Union forces, and then the Confederates pulled back out of Gettysburg.

On July 1, the Confederate army returned and attacked, and more Union forces arrived to join the fight. It was combat at close quarters. Soldiers were fighting with their bayonets, fists, and the butts of their rifles. In the afternoon, a fresh surge of Confederate soldiers was able to drive the Union forces back through Gettysburg and up to Cemetery Hill. By the end of the first day, 9,000 Union soldiers had been killed or wounded.

Fighting intensified the following afternoon farther south along the ridge of Cemetery Hill. General James Longstreet led an attack against the left flank of the Union forces in a rocky valley, while another attack was launched against the right at Culp's Hill. All day long and into the night, the Confederates tried to climb the left flank and Culp's Hill on the right without success. Bodies piled on top of each other until both armies stopped for the day due to exhaustion.

That evening, General Meade received word that Union casualties had exceeded 20,000. Meade predicted that Lee would strike in the morning at the center and moved more men to protect the cemetery ridge. Lee decided that Major General George Pickett's forces would lead a final charge against the center of the line. Fifteen thousand of Pickett's men and 130 cannons were brought into a line just southwest of the town.

Just after noon, the Confederate cannons opened up again, driving Union troops deeper into their trenches. Pickett waited for General Longstreet to order the attack and then could wait no longer. Pickett's men charged up the cemetery ridge just as the last of the Confederate cannonballs was dispensed. Out in the open, Pickett's charge was cut down by Union rifles and cannons. By nightfall, the Confederates were in full retreat, and the patter of rain and the moans of men dying on the grassy hills were the final sounds of the Battle of Gettysburg.

The Horror of War

It is estimated that more than 50,000 men were killed, wounded, missing, or captured during the Battle of Gettysburg. The South had lost one-third of its men and would never be able to threaten the North again.

William C. Robertson's lithograph from 1867 depicts the bloody Battle of Gettysburg.

The morning of July 4, 1863, revealed a horrific scene. The 8,000 dead soldiers and 5,000 dead horses far outnumbered the citizens of Gettysburg. On Cemetery Hill, arms of Union soldiers lay across legs of fallen Confederates. Burial parties of Union soldiers, local citizens, and aid organizations moved quickly to bury the dead before disease spread. Graves were dug no more than 3 feet (0.9 m) deep. The stench of bodies hung in the summer heat over the town.

This twenty-first century photograph shows one of the Ohio monuments in Gettysburg National Military Park in Pennsylvania.

Gettysburg was the first battle in which large numbers of Union soldiers had been killed in Northern territory. Traditionally, burial of wartime dead was left to state and local authorities. However, no one could have predicted that 13,000 bodies would be scattered across this village. On July 24, David Wills, a local businessman and lawyer, wrote to the governor of Pennsylvania about the awful conditions. According to Garry Wills (no relation) in *Lincoln at Gettysburg*, David Wills noted, "In many instances arms and legs and sometimes heads protrude and my attention has been directed to several places where the hogs were actually rooting out the bodies and devouring."

Pennsylvania governor Andrew Curtin authorized Wills to purchase land for a proper cemetery. He also requested assistance from the seventeen states that had lost soldiers at Gettysburg.

Wills formed the National Soldiers' Cemetery Corporation, which was governed by a board composed of one appointee from each state that had lost soldiers. For $2,475.87, Wills bought 17 acres (6.9 hectares). According to Barbara Silberdick Feinberg in *Abraham Lincoln's Gettysburg Address*, Wills described it in an August 17 letter to Curtin:

> The grounds embrace about seventeen acres on Cemetery Hill, fronting the Baltimore turnpike, and extending to the Taneytown road . . . It is the spot which should be specifically consecrated to this sacred purpose. It was here that such immense quantities of our artillery were massed, and during Thursday and Friday of the battle, from this most important position [on] the field, dealt out death and destruction to the rebel army in every direction of their advance.

The Board of Governors decided to hire William Saunders. He was the superintendent of grounds in the Department of Agriculture and a leading architect in the popular "rural cemetery" movement. With city populations increasing, moving city cemeteries to the country freed precious space and placed the dead in a more natural and peaceful environment. Saunders presented his design to the president and, according to Garry Wills in *Lincoln at Gettysburg*, he recalled in a later journal, "He [Lincoln] was much pleased with the method of the graves, said it differed from the ordinary cemetery, and, after I had explained the reasons, said it was an advisable and benefitting arrangement."

In his plan, Saunders arranged the graves in a half-circle around a central monument to be built later. Honored with individual tombstones, the dead of each state were grouped together, with a 4-foot (1.2 m) walkway between sections, and headed by a large, uniform tombstone. No state was given preference over another, and no area was marked for Confederate dead, many of whom were later buried in the South.

As the Union soldiers were taken from their shallow graves and moved to the new cemetery site, Wills started to make arrangements for a proper ceremony to dedicate the grounds of what would become known as the bloodiest battle in the Civil War.

CHAPTER THREE

THE CEREMONY AT THE SOLDIERS' NATIONAL CEMETERY

After the Battle of Gettysburg, on July 1 through July 3, 1863, the women and men of the town of Gettysburg used peppermint oil under their noses. The stench of dead humans and animals was nauseating. The hot summer air intensified the smell. Because the battle had created such great losses, digging proper graves was difficult.

David Wills wanted the cemetery ceremony to be consecrated by a great speaker. Lincoln was not his first choice. Wills could not know, however, that Lincoln's speech would be what history remembered most about that day.

Possible Orators for the Event

Before the cemetery was dug, Wills felt that the land should be dedicated with a procession to the grounds, gun salutes, music, and speeches. Everyone knew that the foremost American speaker of the time was Edward Everett. A former US senator,

This photograph shows the view from Cemetary Ridge in Gettysburg.

governor of Massachusetts, secretary of state, and minister (ambassador) to Britain, Everett had had a distinguished career in public service. He accepted Wills's invitation.

A printed circular was distributed to important leaders around the North. While it is not known if President Lincoln received one, he did send a note indicating that he would attend. The Board of Governors faced a problem: should

Lincoln be invited to speak, too? According to Feinberg in *Abraham Lincoln's Gettysburg Address*, Clark Carr, Illinois's representative to the board, said, "The question was raised as to his ability to speak upon such a grave and solemn occasion." Although he was a capable speaker, Lincoln's humor came from the rural Midwest, and there was some concern that his speech would be too informal. However, on November 2, Wills sent a letter to Lincoln asking him to stay at Wills's home in Gettysburg and to make a "few appropriate remarks" at the ceremony, "We hope you will be able to be present to perform this last solemn act to the Soldiers dead on this Battle Field."

The large audience and the gathered dignitaries presented an opportunity for the president to rally support for continuing this long and costly war. In waging war, Lincoln's first goal was keeping the Union together, and he wanted to use the opportunity to remind the country of that goal.

The Myth of Lincoln's Writing Process

There is considerable debate over when Lincoln wrote the speech that would become the Gettysburg Address. Some scholars have suggested that he dashed off the speech while on the train to Gettysburg or that evening in his room at Wills's house. However, John Nicolay, one of his personal secretaries, noted in his diary that Lincoln used "great deliberation in arranging his thoughts and moulding his phrases, mentally, waiting to reduce them to writing 'til they had taken satisfactory form."

It is more likely that Lincoln worked on the speech in the weeks leading up to the ceremony. In the midst of his busy

The room shown above is the Lincoln Sitting Room in the White House.

schedule, Lincoln may have retreated to his second-floor office in the White House to think about his speech.

In the "business wing," as he called it, Lincoln liked to sit at the long table before the windows that overlooked the Potomac. As he regarded the river, 80 miles (129 km) behind which lay the bodies of thousands of American men, Lincoln may have contemplated how to phrase his "few appropriate remarks." As the featured speaker, Everett was expected to deliver a lengthy discussion of what had happened at the battle, setting the scene in exact detail. Although Lincoln had good knowledge of the events at Gettysburg from the War Department, he knew that the short remarks required of him as president needed to examine the largest issue on the minds of his audience: why were they still fighting this war?

To preserve the Union was Lincoln's first goal, so he could not cast blame on the South. His speech had to find a more timeless tone. A reader of the classics, Lincoln had a strong sense for the rhythmic language of great writing. With the opportunity to speak at such an important occasion, it is likely that Lincoln worked carefully on his speech over a period of weeks.

On November 15, Lincoln confided to Noah Brooks, a journalist with whom he was friendly, that the Gettysburg speech had been written "but not finished." At noon on November 18, Lincoln boarded a special four-car train for the trip to Gettysburg. John Nicolay reported in his memoir that Lincoln had written the first nineteen lines on Executive Mansion paper without corrections to the page; it is likely that earlier drafts of the speech had existed.

Decked in red, white, and blue bunting and American flags, the train stopped at many stations to collect officials and dignitaries. As the train approached Gettysburg, Lincoln excused himself and retreated to the drawing room in the back of the last car to continue work on his speech.

The Ceremony

In the late afternoon, the William Mason locomotive pulled into the station on Carlisle Street in a very crowded town. For days, people had been pouring into Gettysburg by train, by buggy, or on foot. Crude seats had been placed into the boxcars of freight trains. Piled at the station were the wooden coffins provided by the federal government. There was going to be a large crowd for this somber occasion.

A layer of low clouds hung over the town of Gettysburg on the morning of November 19, suggesting rain. Before the procession assembled for the short march to the cemetery, the sky had begun to clear. At 10 a.m., President Lincoln stepped onto Carlisle Street wearing a black suit, white gloves, and a black silk top hat with a band around it. The band was a sign of mourning for his son Willie, who had died of a fever the year before. When Lincoln mounted the chestnut horse large enough for his tall frame, he towered above the procession and onlookers.

The procession left from the town square at 11 a.m. Four military bands were scattered throughout the parade and played funeral music. With so much effort placed on burying the dead, the people of Gettysburg had yet to repair their fences or to clear their lands of toppled trees.

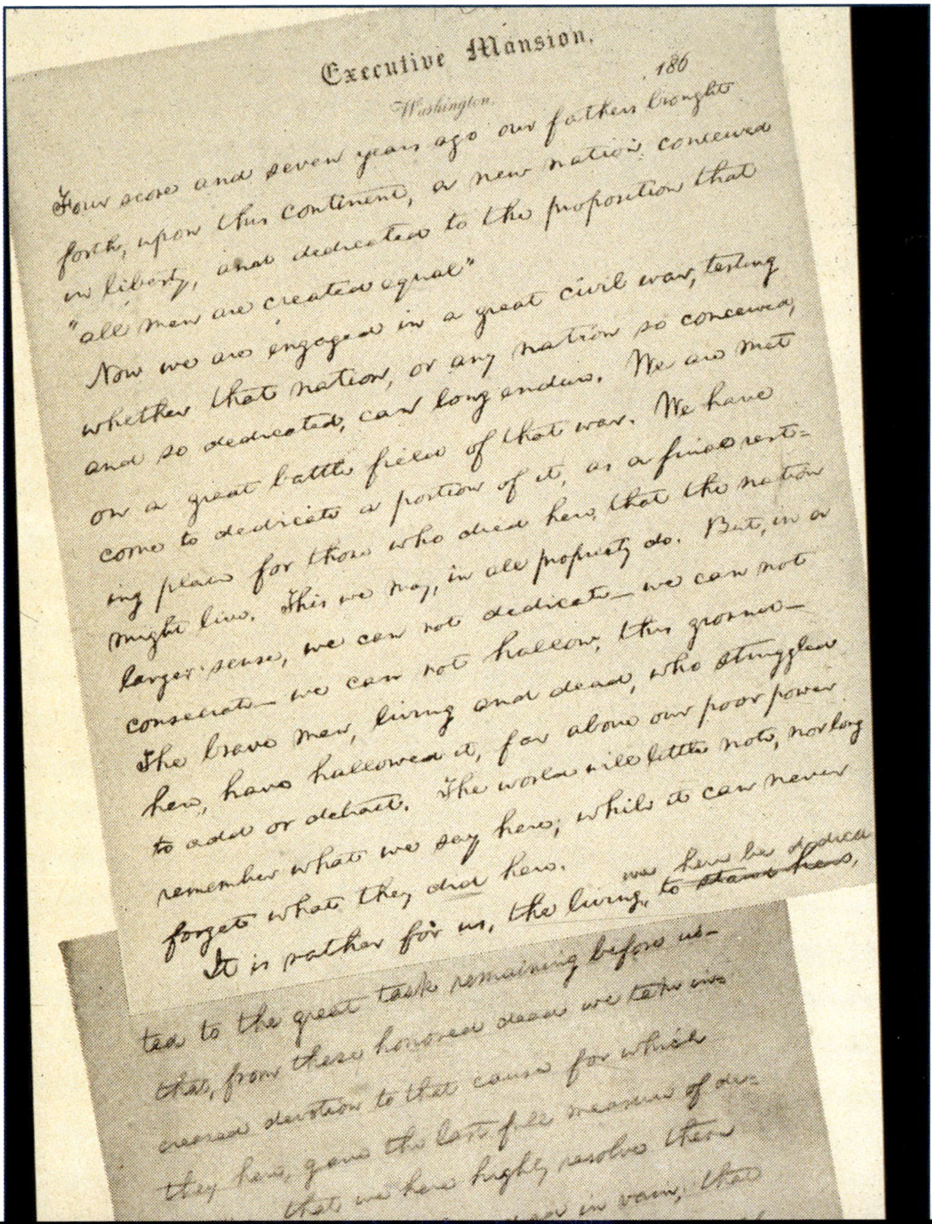
Executive Mansion,
Washington, 186
Four score and seven years ago our fathers brought forth, upon this continent, a new nation, conceived in liberty, and dedicated to the proposition that "all men are created equal"
Now we are engaged in a great civil war, testing whether that nation, or any nation so conceived, and so dedicated, can long endure. We are met on a great battle field of that war. We have come to dedicate a portion of it, as a final resting place for those who died here, that the nation might live. This we may, in all propriety do. But, in a larger sense, we can not dedicate—we can not consecrate—we can not hallow, this ground— The brave men, living and dead, who struggled here, have hallowed it, far above our poor power to add or detract. The world will little note, nor long remember what we say here; while it can never forget what they did here.
It is rather for us, the living, we here be dedicated to the great task remaining before us— that, from these honored dead we take increased devotion to that cause for which they here, gave the last full measure of de
that we here highly resolve them
in vain, that

Here is a draft of the Gettysburg Address, which President Lincoln wrote on Executive Mansion stationary. "Executive Mansion" was the official name for the White House between 1810 and 1902.

Versions of the Gettysburg Address

There is some mystery about the drafts of the Gettysburg Address. Historians know that after Lincoln wrote the first drafts, he gave one to his secretary, John Nicolay and one to his other secretary, John Hay. Nicolay said that Lincoln used his draft at the ceremony. The Hay draft stayed with the Hay family until 1906.

After the event, the organizer, David Wills, asked Lincoln for a copy of his speech for official records. This copy was never returned.

Another copy was created for Edward Everett. Everett already had a draft of the address but he wanted this version for a book for auction.

The last copy, the Bliss copy, is the most commonly reproduced version today. It is also the one this book uses. Lincoln wrote this copy for Colonel Alexander Bliss.

At the cemetery, the crowd had swelled in advance of the arriving dignitaries. Only one-third of the bodies had been buried, and open graves drew curious onlookers. On the 3 foot (0.9 m) platform, President Lincoln settled between Secretary of State William Seward and the seat reserved for Edward Everett, who arrived one hour late.

After the opening prayer, Everett rose, bowed to the president, and began:

> Standing beneath this serene sky, overlooking these broad fields now reposing from the labors of the waning year, the mighty Alleghenies dimly towering before us, the graves of our brethren beneath our feet, it is with hesitation that I raise my poor voice to break the eloquent silence of God and Nature.

A skilled orator, Everett was famous for his beautiful voice and colorful expression. Everett had completely memorized his 13,000-word speech. He described local sites in detail. He knew the names of the officers involved. At times, his speech became poetic, recalling the rites of the Greeks to honor their dead. He spoke for two hours, which was not unusual for the time.

When Everett returned to his seat under a rain of applause, Ward Lamon, Lincoln's personal bodyguard, got up to introduce the president. Lincoln rose. According to Feinberg in *Abraham Lincoln's Gettysburg Address*, E. W. Andrews, a reverend, noted from the crowd, "President Lincoln was so put together physically that, to him, gracefulness of movement was an impossibility. But his awkwardness was lost sight of in the interest which the expression of his face and what he said awakened."

Unlike Everett's sweet voice, Lincoln spoke in an almost squeaky manner that still contained a bit of a Kentucky accent. At the podium, he removed from his pocket his glasses and the two sheets of paper containing his speech. Directly in front of him stood an honor guard of Union soldiers, some with gruesome wounds. He had to have something suitable to say to them.

Before the photographer was able to set up his camera to capture the moment, Lincoln's speech was over. According to John Nicolay, he stopped five times for applause yet concluded in just a few minutes. A funeral song played as the crowd thought about what had been said. The Reverend H. L. Baugher gave the benediction to conclude the event. The crowd exited peaceably.

After attending a meeting at the local Presbyterian church, Lincoln boarded his train that evening and returned to Washington. Exhausted from a long day, the president, suffering from a headache, sprawled across a bench in the last car.

CHAPTER FOUR

THE SPEECH

Lincoln may not have realized the worth of his speech immediately after he gave it. First, he was sick. When he returned to Washington, the next day, Lincoln was ill and diagnosed with varioloid, a less dangerous form of smallpox. Lincoln had to stay in the White House for the next three weeks. His speech was out in the world and many people were reacting to it, both positively and negatively.

Response to Lincoln's Speech

Most newspaper accounts of the ceremony focused on Everett's lengthy speech. Even among witnesses of the event, there was disagreement on Lincoln's effect on the crowd. Reliable sources heaped praise on the president for his fine remarks. According to the *Chicago Tribune*, "The dedicatory remarks by President Lincoln will live among the annals of man." To the *Springfield Republican*, Lincoln's speech was "deep in feeling, compact in thought and expression, and tasteful and elegant in every word and comma." George William Curtis of *Harper's Weekly* noted, "The few words from the President were from the heart to the heart."

This photograph is from the view of the crowd at the Gettysburg Address.

Yet many responded to the address as a political tool of Lincoln's troubled presidency. The *Richmond Examiner*, a major newspaper in Virginia, called the event a "stage play" with a "vein of comedy." In the *Chicago Times*, a newspaper with connections to the Democratic Party, Lincoln's speech was ridiculed: "The cheek of every American must tingle with

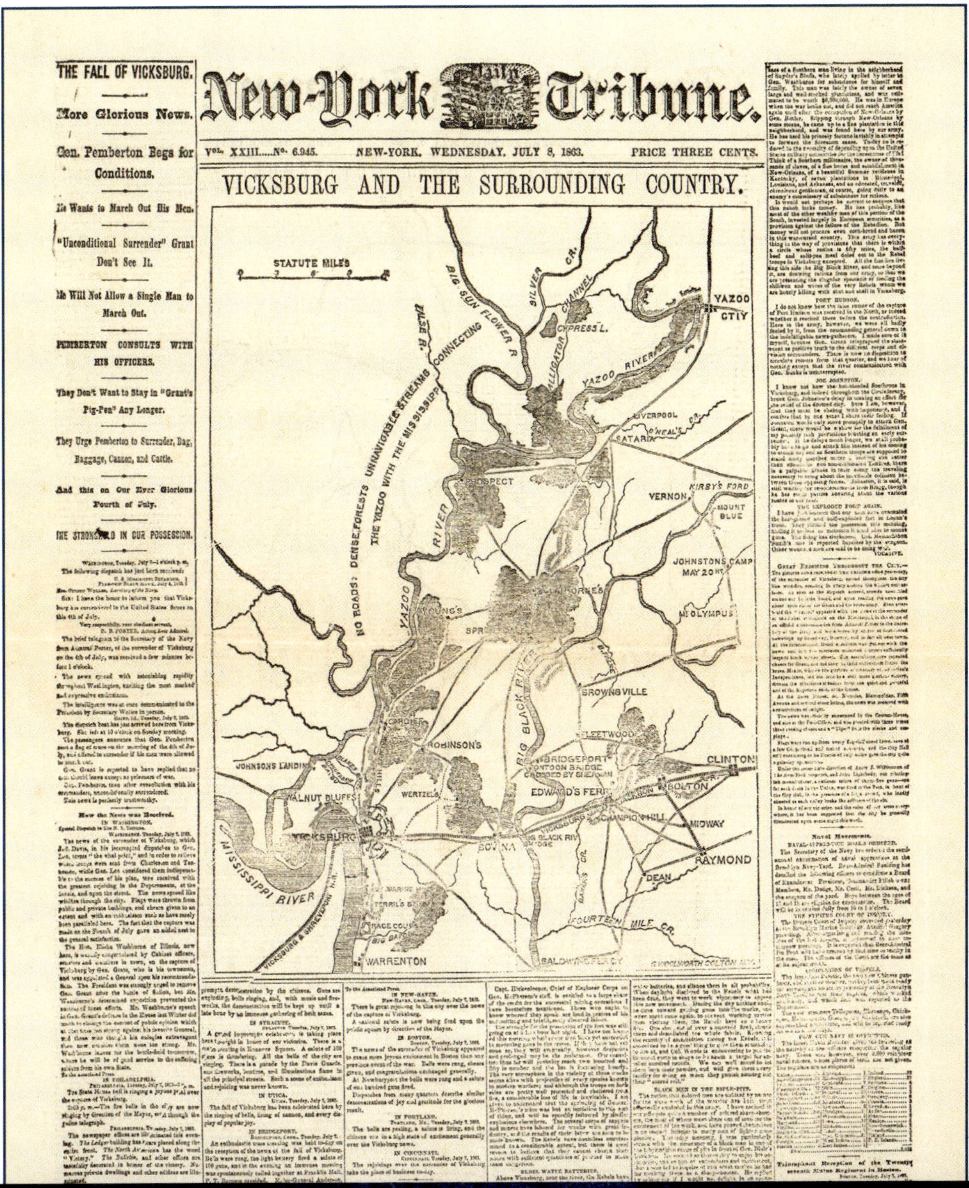

THE FALL OF VICKSBURG.

More Glorious News.

Gen. Pemberton Begs for Conditions.

He Wants to March Out His Men.

"Unconditional Surrender" Grant Don't See It.

He Will Not Allow a Single Man to March Out.

PEMBERTON CONSULTS WITH HIS OFFICERS.

They Don't Want to Stay in "Grant's Pig-Pen" Any Longer.

They Urge Pemberton to Surrender, Bag, Baggage, Cannon, and Cattle.

And this on Our Ever Glorious Fourth of July.

THE STRONGHOLD IN OUR POSSESSION.

New-York Daily Tribune.

VOL. XXIII.....No. 6,945. NEW-YORK, WEDNESDAY, JULY 8, 1863. PRICE THREE CENTS.

VICKSBURG AND THE SURROUNDING COUNTRY.

This map from the *New York Tribune* shows the Battle of Gettysburg.

shame as he reads the silly, flat, and dish-watery utterances of the man . . . " These writers examined the speech as an instrument of a Republican president struggling to secure another term, not as the president's dream of a brighter future far from the bloody fields of war.

Lincoln's Writing Process

According to Lincoln's personal secretary, John Nicolay, Lincoln's writing process was as follows: he liked to take large amounts of information (he read constantly) and then condense them down into small, palpable ideas. He spent hours drafting and reworking speeches and although he complained that he did not have adequate time to write the Gettysburg Address, he presumably thought about it considerably. On the train ride to Gettysburg, he may have been thinking about his ending, which he had a hard time figuring out. Historians know he started the Nicolay draft in Washington, DC, because it was written on Executive Mansion stationary. Lincoln was a deep, thoughtful thinker and part of what's so impressive about the address is how he manages to take complex ideas like those in the Declaration of Independence and condense them down into an almost haiku-like speech.

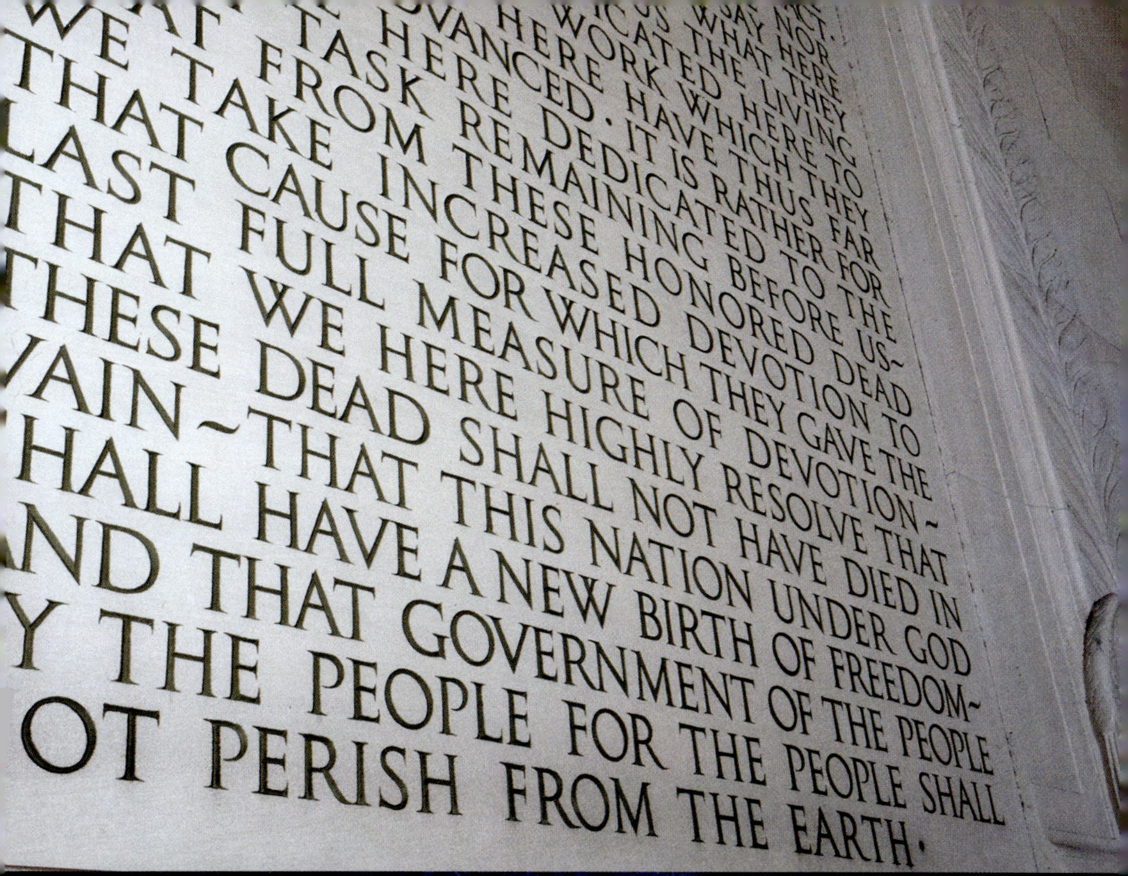

The Gettysburg Address is written on the walls of the Lincoln Memorial in Washington, DC.

The Meaning of the Speech

What did Lincoln intend to communicate with these 272 words spoken on a clear morning in Pennsylvania? In his speech, he did not even mention Pennsylvania. Nor did he mention the town of Gettysburg. He mentioned neither a North nor a South and assigned no blame for the battle. In failing to name any events, dates, or places, Lincoln gave his speech a timeless quality. As much as his address was directed to the 20,000 people

Congress of the United States, begun and held at the City of New-York, on Wednesday the fourth of March, one thousand seven hundred and eighty nine.

Above is the Bill of Rights, which includes the Tenth Amendment, an amendment that protects states' rights.

gathered at Gettysburg, it was also addressed to Americans of the future.

What, then, was Lincoln attempting to communicate to the people in front of him and to the political leaders on the stage with him? What was he trying to say to the nation as a whole—and to the people who might be reading it more than 150 years later?

The Gettysburg Address begins, "Four score and seven years ago our fathers brought forth on this continent, a new nation, conceived in Liberty, and dedicated to the proposition that all men are created equal."

Speaking in 1863, Lincoln began by drawing the attention of his listeners to a significant occasion of the past. The word "score" is an old-fashioned way of referring to twenty. Therefore, "four score" means eighty. Eighty-seven years before 1863 was 1776, the year when the Declaration of Independence was signed. Lincoln was suggesting that the nation was born with the signing of the Declaration of Independence.

Why is this significant? One of the main arguments behind the Confederacy's secession from the Union was in the Tenth Amendment. The Tenth Amendment was part of the Bill of Rights in the United States Constitution, which was signed eleven years after the Declaration of Independence. By mentioning this earlier document, Lincoln was asking his audience to look at the Declaration of Independence, instead of the Constitution, for the meaning of the United States.

Lincoln's words meant that in 1776, our fathers founded a nation in which "all men are created equal." Since the writing of the Declaration of Independence, the meaning of that phrase had been debated and fought over. After all, many of the signers of the declaration, including Lincoln's hero Thomas Jefferson, owned slaves, yet the slaves were not freed with the signing of the document. Although Lincoln had freed slaves in the Confederacy with the Emancipation Proclamation earlier in the year, they had not yet become free people. In the North, Lincoln received constant pressure to emphasize that the reason for fighting the war was to keep the Union together and not to free the slaves. Indeed, Lincoln himself would have agreed that the first goal above all others was to keep the Union together. Why then would the president place this statement in his speech, angering many potential supporters?

In an 1859 letter to Henry L. Pierce, Lincoln honored Thomas Jefferson, the writer of the Declaration of Independence:

> All honor to Jefferson—to the man who, in the concrete pressure of a struggle for national independence by a single person, had the coolness, forecast, and capacity to introduce into a merely revolutionary document, an abstract truth, applicable to all men and all times, and so to embalm it there, that today, and in all coming days, it shall be a rebuke and a stumbling-block to the very harbingers of reappearing tyranny and oppression.

In adding the phrase "all men are created equal" to the Gettysburg Address, Lincoln had placed a similar "abstract truth." In referring to Jefferson's phrase,

Lincoln was suggesting that imperfect as America may have been, Americans could always look to improve the nation to approach the ideal of equality for all men, as defined at America's birth.

Lincoln's hero, Thomas Jefferson, is shown above.

In the lines, "Now we are engaged in a great civil war, testing whether that nation, or any nation so conceived and so dedicated, can long endure," Lincoln addressed the issue of the day. He equated the Civil War to a "testing" of "that nation," a nation not divided into North and South. In this test, Lincoln seemed to ask, would this creation known as the United States survive? Standing at the location where 50,000 men were killed, wounded, missing, or captured over a period of three days, Lincoln asked his audience to look away from the bloodshed to the larger issue of whether the United States could survive. While Everett's speech examined the specific events of the battle, Lincoln focused his remarks on

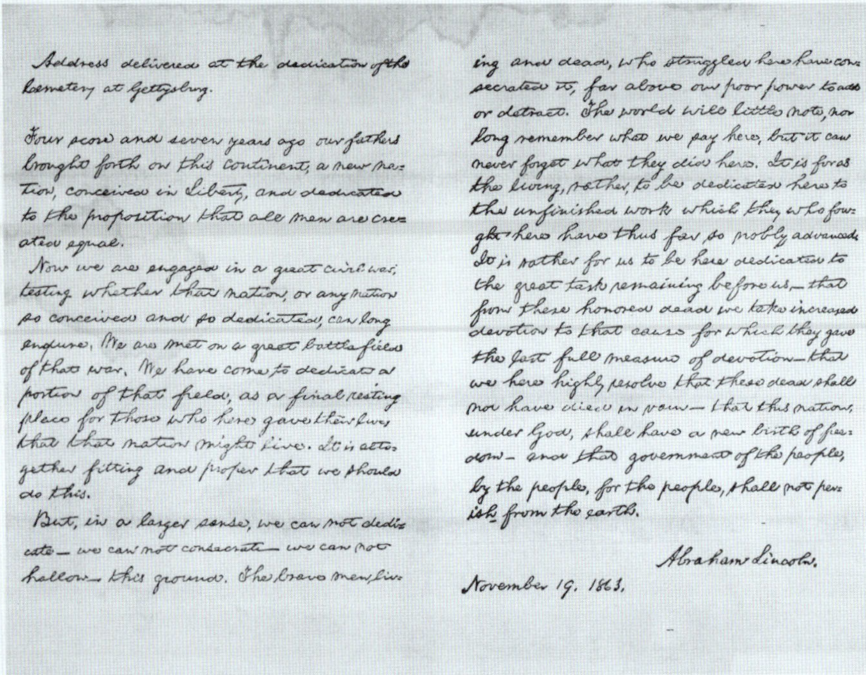

Address delivered at the dedication of the Cemetery at Gettysburg.

Four score and seven years ago our fathers brought forth on this continent, a new nation, conceived in Liberty, and dedicated to the proposition that all men are created equal.

Now we are engaged in a great civil war, testing whether that nation, or any nation so conceived and so dedicated, can long endure. We are met on a great battle-field of that war. We have come to dedicate a portion of that field, as a final resting place for those who here gave their lives, that that nation might live. It is altogether fitting and proper that we should do this.

But, in a larger sense, we can not dedicate — we can not consecrate — we can not hallow — this ground. The brave men, living and dead, who struggled here have consecrated it, far above our poor power to add or detract. The world will little note, nor long remember what we say here, but it can never forget what they did here. It is for us the living, rather, to be dedicated here to the unfinished work which they who fought here have thus far so nobly advanced. It is rather for us to be here dedicated to the great task remaining before us — that from these honored dead we take increased devotion to that cause for which they gave the last full measure of devotion — that we here highly resolve that these dead shall not have died in vain — that this nation, under God, shall have a new birth of freedom — and that government of the people, by the people, for the people, shall not perish from the earth.

Abraham Lincoln.

November 19. 1863.

Here is a lithograph of the Gettysburg Address.

the ideals represented by the battle, a fitting gesture for the president of the nation.

Lincoln states,"We are met on a great battle-field of that war. We have come to dedicate a portion of that field, as a final resting place for those who here gave their lives that that nation might live. It is altogether fitting and proper that we should do this." In three sentences in a row, Lincoln used "we" as the subject. While the use of "we" was directed to the audience before him at Gettysburg, it also applied to the nation as a whole. He was saying that "we," the nation, must review this "great battle-field" in this "great civil war." By repeating "we" and "great," Lincoln added a musical quality to his speech, and like a song or poem, it lifted his audience's attention to the task of honoring those who sacrificed their lives at Gettysburg. Their sacrifices were tied to the nation's struggle for greatness, and as president, Lincoln honored them. Lincoln states, "But in a larger sense, we cannot dedicate—we cannot consecrate—we cannot hallow—this ground. The brave men, living and dead, who struggled here, have consecrated it, far above our power to add or detract." These words showed that Lincoln recognized that those at the ceremony could not make the grounds sacred, as the dead men had already done so. In many respects, Lincoln was humble and very aware that the presidency was greater than any man who bore the title. He modestly, yet inaccurately states,"The world will little note, nor long remember what we say here, but it can never forget what they did here. It is for us the living, rather, to be dedicated here to the unfinished work which they who fought here have thus far so nobly advanced."

Lincoln began to move forward in time to the future, suggesting that the memories created by the event would be stronger than any words used to describe them. He then challenged his audience to be dedicated to the "unfinished work" of the men who had fought to determine that the United States, conceived under the notion that all men are created equal, would survive. The fight had to go on, Lincoln argued, and the steady repetition of the term "here" demanded of his audience that it should decide at that moment to continue the fight.

> It is rather for us to be here dedicated to the great task remaining before us—that from these honored dead we take increased devotion to that cause for which they gave the last full measure of devotion—that we here highly resolve that these dead shall not have died in vain—that this nation, under God, shall have a new birth of freedom—and that government of the people, by the people, for the people, shall not perish from the earth.

Here, Lincoln spoke of the need to pick up the cause for which the dead had given their lives, their "last full measure of devotion." He pointed in the direction of the battle, where the nation "shall have a new birth of freedom." In repeating the word "nation" five times in his speech, Lincoln underlined that the Union and Confederacy were never to be divided. Lincoln suggested that a victory by the North would result in the birth of a new nation. Its government would be "of the people, by the people, for the people." While the nation had yet to meet the ideal that all men are created equal, Lincoln painted a future ideal, a new goal, in which the government finally represented the people of the nation, all of them, whether they stood before him on that November morning in Gettysburg or read his words from a book nearly eight score years later.

CHAPTER FIVE

AN ENDURING DOCUMENT

Lincoln was pleased by the outcome of the Battle of Gettysburg. However, he quickly became angry by the actions of the north. General Meade, the Northern general, did not follow Robert E. Lee's army across the Potomac River and into Virginia. Meade said that his army was weak. They needed to bury the men who had died at Gettysburg. Lincoln was disappointed by Meade's decision. He wrote to a colleague, "Our army held the war in the hollow of their hand and they would not close it." Lincoln knew that the coming months would be challenging. The war would continue.

The War Finally Ends

The war carried on for another eighteen months. A year after Gettysburg, General William T. Sherman's army captured Atlanta and began its famous march to the sea. As the tide of the war turned in favor of the Union, Lincoln's popularity rose. He was reelected in a landslide victory in November 1864. In January of the following year, Congress passed the

Abraham Lincoln stands with soldiers at Antietam in 1862.

Thirteenth Amendment, which, when ratified, abolished the institution of slavery. On April 9, 1865, General Robert E. Lee surrendered the Army of Northern Virginia, the last unit of the Confederacy still fighting, in Appomattox Court House, Virginia. The bloodiest war in American history ended, with approximately 650,000 dead.

Five days later, President Lincoln was shot dead in Ford's Theatre in Washington, DC, by actor John Wilkes Booth. The

This photo collage shows the US senators who voted yes to the Thirteenth Amendment.

final casualty of the war, the sixteenth president of the United States died the next day.

Free At Last

As Lincoln predicted, it would be a struggle for America to reach the ideal expressed in the Declaration of Independence and in the Gettysburg Address of equality for all men. Today, many question if we have reached it yet.

In the years following the end of the war, there were attempts to heal the scars in the South, where all of the war's

Preserving the Document

The American Library of Congress has two drafts of the Gettysburg Address. Because paper can so easily biodegrade, the curators have to take careful measures in order to preserve the documents. They use a series of preservation techniques to ensure that the document stays the way it is. One is putting the document between plexiglass panels in steel frames and then rather than keeping oxygen between the glass and the paper, they use the gas argon. The oxygen would erode the paper, so curators have to be careful to only use argon. Visitors can see both the front and the back of the paper and can read Lincoln's elegant handwriting.

battles were fought except for Gettysburg. Between 1865 and 1877, federal troops were stationed in the South in an effort to protect the newly freed African Americans. Congress passed the Fourteenth and Fifteenth Amendments to the Constitution, intending to provide civil and voting rights for them. However, state governments in the South began to enact what later became known as Jim Crow laws. Named after an offensive skit performed by a white actor, these laws restricted business ownership, availability of services, voting rights, and marriage for African Americans and other nonwhites.

In 1878, federal troops were pulled out of the South, several federal government bureaus closed, and the state governments were back in Southern hands. In several states, African Americans were forced to pay a special tax, called a poll tax, to vote. Few could afford to pay it.

Jim Crow laws were not restricted to the South; they were passed in states from Delaware to California. Other kinds of race-based laws were passed well into the twentieth century. As late as 1945, during World War II, Japanese American citizens along the West Coast were rounded up and taken to remote camps because of their ancestry. American women of all colors have suffered as well and were denied the right to vote until 1920.

The road that Lincoln first described at Gettysburg was indeed long. On December 1, 1955, a forty-two-year-old seamstress named Rosa Parks was arrested for refusing to give up her bus seat to a white man and move to the “colored” section at the back of the bus in Montgomery, Alabama. The civil rights movement was born.

Here, a suffragette protests voting restrictions for women.

Inspired by Martin Luther King Jr. and Mahatma Gandhi, the movement struggled for equality for all through civil disobedience. Instead of fighting with guns or fists, civil rights activists, both black people and white people, both Northerners and Southerners, let themselves be arrested, beaten, teargassed, and sometimes killed as their means of fighting for the ideals of which Lincoln spoke. Despite the mistreatment, these brave soldiers marched on, arm in arm, inspired by the powerful words of their leaders.

In 1963, King stood at the Lincoln Memorial where he had led the largest civil rights rally in American history. He began his speech, "Five score years ago, a great American, in

Martin Luther King Jr. and other leaders sit in Washington, DC in front of the Lincoln memorial.

whose symbolic shadow we stand signed the Emancipation Proclamation." In recalling Lincoln's acts of 100 years before, Reverend King painted a new future in his famous "I Have a Dream" speech, "We will be able to speed up that day when all of God's children, black men and white men, Jews and Gentiles, Protestants and Catholics, will be able to join hands and sing . . . Free at last, Free at last, Thank God Almighty, we are free at last."

In 1964, Congress passed the Twenty-Fourth Amendment, which guaranteed that all citizens of age could vote. Like Lincoln before them, Martin Luther King Jr. and Malcolm X, another civil rights leader, were assassinated for their commitment to the struggle for equality. They became sacrifices in the great test of the American ideal that all men are created equal.

Has America reached the end of the road to which President Lincoln pointed? Are all men, women, and children treated equally in America? Recent American events reveal continuing violence against and denial of rights to Americans based on race, color, disability, religious belief, or sexual orientation. In dozens of predominantly African American neighborhoods, there is little trust in the police to protect citizens. Across the country, the LGBTQ+ community struggles to acquire the same rights as heterosexuals. Disabled Americans continue to fight for equal access to services. While advancements have been made, equality for all in a government of the people, by the people, and for the people has yet to reach every part of the laws, governments, and minds of this nation.

There is still work to be done.

PRIMARY SOURCE TRANSCRIPTION

The Gettysburg Address

Four score and seven years ago our fathers brought forth on this continent, a new nation, conceived in Liberty, and dedicated to the proposition that all men are created equal.

Now we are engaged in a great civil war, testing whether that nation, or any nation so conceived and so dedicated, can long endure. We are met on a great battle-field of that war. We have come to dedicate a portion of that field, as a final resting place for those who here gave their lives that that nation might live. It is altogether fitting and proper that we should do this.

But in a larger sense, we cannot dedicate—we cannot consecrate—we cannot hallow—this ground. The brave men, living and dead, who struggled here, have consecrated it, far above our power to add or detract. The world will little note, nor long remember what we say here, but it can never forget what they did here. It is for us the living, rather, to be dedicated here to the unfinished work which they who fought here have thus far so nobly advanced. It is rather for us to be here dedicated to the great task remaining before us—that from these honored dead we take increased devotion to that cause for which they gave the last full measure of devotion—that we here highly resolve that these dead shall not have died in vain—that this nation, under God, shall have a new birth of freedom—and that government of the people, by the people, for the people, shall not perish from the earth.

CHRONOLOGY

1776 July 4: The Declaration of Independence is adopted, and the United States becomes a nation.

1787 November 18: The Constitution of the United States is completed, establishing a formal national government.

1789 September 25: The first ten amendments to the United States Constitution are passed by Congress and known as the Bill of Rights.

1860 November 6: Lincoln is elected the sixteenth president of the United States.

1861 April 12: At 4:30 a.m., Confederate guns fire shots at Fort Sumter in South Carolina, starting the Civil War.

1862 September 22: In a meeting with his cabinet, President Lincoln releases the preliminary Emancipation Proclamation, which would free all slaves in the Confederate states January 1, 1863, if fighting did not stop.

1863 July 1–3: The Battle of Gettysburg is fought in a small Pennsylvania town. With more than 50,000 casualties, it is the bloodiest battle of the Civil War.

1863 July 24: David Wills, a Gettysburg lawyer and businessman, writes to Pennsylvania governor Andrew Curtin to propose the establishment of a national cemetery for the dead at Gettysburg.

1863 September 23: Wills invites Edward Everett, the foremost speaker of his time, to deliver the featured speech at the ceremony dedicating the national cemetery at Gettysburg.

1863 November 2: President Lincoln is invited by Wills to deliver a "few appropriate remarks" at the dedication ceremony.

1863 November 19: Lincoln delivers the Gettysburg Address.

1864 November 8: Lincoln is reelected president in a landslide.

1865 April 9: Confederate general Robert E. Lee surrenders his Army of Northern Virginia to Union general Ulysses S. Grant at Appomattox Court House, Virginia. The Civil War is over.

1865 April 14: President Lincoln is shot by John Wilkes Booth at Ford's Theatre in Washington, DC. He dies the next day.

1865 December 18: The Thirteenth Amendment is ratified, abolishing slavery in the United States.

GLOSSARY

abolition The outlawing of slavery.

biodegrade To decompose.

casualty Someone who is killed in action, wounded, or missing.

civil disobedience Choosing to disobey laws in a nonviolent manner in order to create changes in law or society.

Confederate States of America The group of Southern states that left the United States after the election of Abraham Lincoln as president in 1860.

consecrate To declare or set aside as sacred.

hallow To make holy or to greatly respect.

inter To place a body in a grave, usually with funeral rites.

moderate Having political views that appeal to the widest range of people.

orator A public speaker.

secede To separate from a nation or association.

score A group of twenty.

slavery The practice of owning someone for forced labor.

somber Gloomy.

Union The states of America that remained loyal to President Lincoln and his government during the Civil War.

BIBLIOGRAPHY

Donald, David Herbert. *Lincoln*. New York, NY: Simon & Schuster, 1995.

Feinberg, Barbara Silberdick. *Abraham Lincoln's Gettysburg Address*. Brookfield, CT: The Millbrook Press, 2000.

Goodwin, Doris Kearns. *Team of Rivals: The Political Genius of Abraham Lincoln*. New York, NY: Simon & Schuster, 2005.

Library of Congress. "Gettysburg Address Essay." Gettysburg Address Exhibitions. Retrieved March 27, 2019. https://www.loc.gov/exhibits/gettysburg-address/preservation.html.

Military History Online. "Battle of Gettysburg." 2000. http://www.militaryhistoryonline.com/gettysburg.

Murphy, Jim. *The Long Road to Gettysburg*. New York, NY: Clarion Books, 1992.

Phelan, Mary Kay. *Mr. Lincoln Speaks at Gettysburg*. New York, NY: W. W. Norton and Company, 1966.

Sears, Stephen W. *Gettysburg*. New York, NY: Mariner Books, 2004.

Wills, Garry. *Lincoln at Gettysburg: The Words That Remade America*. New York, NY: Simon & Schuster, 1992.

FURTHER READING

Books

Burleigh, Robert, and Sterling Hundley. *O Captain, My Captain: Walt Whitman, Abraham Lincoln, and the Civil War*. New York, NY: Abrams Books for Young Readers, 2018.

LaPierre, Yvette, and Keli Sipperley. *Living through the Civil War*. Vero Beach, FL: Rourke Educational Media, 2019.

Loh-Hagan, Virginia. *Union Triumph: Battle of Gettysburg*. Ann Arbor, MI: Cherry Lake Publishing, 2019.

Murphy, Frank, and Sarah Green. *Brave Clara Barton*. New York, NY: Random House, 2018.

Randolph, Joanne, and Harold Holzer. *Mr. Lincoln*. New York, NY: PowerKids Press, 2018.

Websites

National Museum of American History

americanhistory.si.edu/blog/2011/04/exploring-the-gettysburg-address-with-kids.html

This website shows ideas and activities, like exploring the interactive document or viewing the battlegrounds of Gettysburg on Google Earth, that will help readers contextualize the Gettysburg Address.

PBS: The Address

www.pbs.org/kenburns/the-address/home

This website allows viewers to watch clips from a Ken Burns documentary about students at a school in Vermont who memorized the Gettysburg Address.

Smithsonian: The Gettysburg Address
americanhistory.si.edu/documentsgallery/exhibitions/gettysburg_address_2.html
This website tells readers the history of the last known draft of the Gettysburg Address and shows photographs from the war.

INDEX